AN IDEAS INTO ACTION GUIDEBOOK

Managing Conflict with Peers

IDEAS INTO ACTION GUIDEBOOKS

Aimed at managers and executives who are concerned with
their own and others' development, each guidebook in this
series gives specific advice on how to complete a developmental
task or solve a leadership problem.

LEAD CONTRIBUTOR	Talula Cartwright
GUIDEBOOK ADVISORY GROUP	Victoria A. Guthrie
	Cynthia D. McCauley
	Ellen Van Velsor
DIRECTOR OF PUBLICATIONS	Martin Wilcox
EDITOR	Peter Scisco
DESIGN AND LAYOUT	Joanne Ferguson
CONTRIBUTING ARTISTS	Laura J. Gibson
	Chris Wilson, 29 & Company

CCL No. 419
ISBN-13: 978-1-932973-93-8
ISBN-10: 1-932973-93-1

CENTER FOR CREATIVE LEADERSHIP
POST OFFICE BOX 26300
GREENSBORO, NORTH CAROLINA 27438-6300
336-288-7210 • WWW.CCL.ORG/PUBLICATIONS

AN IDEAS INTO ACTION GUIDEBOOK

Managing Conflict with Peers

Talula Cartwright

Center for
Creative
Leadership

NORTH AMERICA EUROPE ASIA

www.ccl.org

THE IDEAS INTO ACTION GUIDEBOOK SERIES

This series of guidebooks draws on the practical knowledge that the Center for Creative Leadership (CCL®) has generated, since its inception in 1970, through its research and educational activity conducted in partnership with hundreds of thousands of managers and executives. Much of this knowledge is shared—in a way that is distinct from the typical university department, professional association, or consultancy. CCL is not simply a collection of individual experts, although the individual credentials of its staff are impressive; rather it is a community, with its members holding certain principles in common and working together to understand and generate practical responses to today's leadership and organizational challenges.

The purpose of the series is to provide managers with specific advice on how to complete a developmental task or solve a leadership challenge. In doing that, the series carries out CCL's mission to advance the understanding, practice, and development of leadership for the benefit of society worldwide. We think you will find the Ideas Into Action Guidebooks an important addition to your leadership toolkit.

Table of Contents

Executive Brief

A great many peer conflicts arise from incompatible goals or from different views on how a task should be accomplished. With honest dialogue these kinds of conflicts can usually be resolved. But other peer conflicts are more troublesome because they involve personal values, office politics and power, and emotional reactions.

To resolve these more difficult peer conflicts, managers should examine three key issues that can cause such clashes and also influence their outcome. One, they should assess their emotional "hot buttons" that trigger ineffective behaviors and make conflict difficult to manage. Two, they should examine their personal values and how those might conflict with what their peers find important. Finally, they should assess their power in the organization—which can be related to position, influence, expertise, or some other factor —and learn how to use it to manage conflicts.

Navigating these issues won't rid an organization of conflict among peers. But by paying attention to them managers can build effective relationships that will survive these inevitable conflicts and bolster their ability to achieve organizational goals.

Is Conflict Destructive?

When professional peers work as independent contributors or together as teams in an organization, conflicts are bound to occur. This is especially true in today's flatter organizations, where managers depend on peer relationships to get their work done. When people have compatible goals, a predictable structure, and harmonious relationships, conflicts are fewer. In the traditional military, for example, a deliberate intention to reduce conflict among soldiers and their leaders is made by using structured hierarchies and communication channels designed to settle conflicts before they occur. The looser the organizational structure is, the more harmonious the relationships have to be to avoid conflicts. In a group of social peers, for example, there might be fewer conflicts simply because the people like each other so much. In a long-standing work team, conflicts may be fewer because the team members have gotten to know each other over a period of time.

Inevitably, though, no matter how harmonious the group or how structured the organization, conflicts are bound to occur. Some conflicts may feel unproductive, even destructive. Peer conflicts can have high stakes because often your peers have the ear of your boss, and in a future management shuffle may in fact become your boss. Effective managers know that conflicts with their peers can't really be avoided and learn to understand and resolve them.

Often how you feel about a conflict depends on your perspective and how comfortable you are in conflict situations. If you're having a conflict with a peer about how to accomplish a goal, for example, often that conflict can enhance the thinking process and bring better results because both of you voice different opinions and avoid "groupthink"—the tendency for group members to think alike. Many people actually enjoy this kind of intellectual conflict and find it invigorating. Others find this kind of conflict uncomfortable, even to the point of not participating in these kinds of discussions and so depriving the team and the organization of their insights and ideas. With training and some experience, however, they can learn to handle such conflict situations with good results.

When conflict involves more than ideas—when it becomes emotional—handling the situation is harder. The reason emotional conflict situations are so uncomfortable is that they touch something deep inside, something that is part of your history, something that is very sensitive or tender.

Have you ever thought about how you feel about conflict? Conflict between peers—in fact, any conflict between two people—often triggers an emotional response. When emotions come into play they can affect your skill at managing conflict and also influence the outcome of the conflict. By learning how you react emotionally to conflict and developing sensitivity to the emotional responses of your peers, you can increase your effectiveness at resolving conflict. Without that awareness and empathy, a conflict of ideas can be overwhelmed by emotions or degenerate into bad feelings and re-criminations. Your goals in managing conflict with peers should always include strengthening your working relationships in addition to negotiating the issue in dispute.

A Process for Managing Conflict

Each of your peers may have different feelings about conflict from you, but that doesn't mean that you have to develop a different conflict manage-ment process for each of them. Becoming aware of these differences and the impact they have on conflicts will help you resolve disagreements more effectively than if you just trade favors. Such horse-trading might deliver a solution, but it won't do much to turn a peer conflict into an effective and more productive working relationship.

The nature of peer relationships can sometimes make a conflict management process difficult to implement. You and your peers likely occupy equal but different positions in the organization. Because contemporary organizations rely so heavily on peer relationships to achieve results (command and control hierarchies giving way to collaborative, horizontal networks), using a conflict management process that relies on partnership can be a successful strategy for reaching resolution. A collaborative conflict management process focuses on finding an underlying common principle that you and your peer can agree on. From that common point both of you can move toward a resolution. Because peer relationships often continue for some time, if either side of a conflict feels a loss the relationship can be damaged and the organization loses—it misses out on the productivity, innovation, and implementation that effective work relationships bring.

Think about a conflict you have now or have recently had with a peer. Is there a common principle (for example, the best interests of the company or your department) that the two of you can or could have agreed on? What can you do, or what could you have done, to manage the conflict to achieve that result?

You move a long way toward answering those questions, and toward more effectively managing conflict with your peers, by considering more fully who your peers are (how they respond to specific emotional triggers, what they value, what kind of organizational power they have) and who you are (your responses, your values, your power). That knowledge gives you a better idea of what your conflicts are likely to be about and what the stakes are. The following guidelines introduce themes that are common to successful conflict management. They draw on your strengths as a manager—problem solving and technical skills—and add to those strengths an awareness of conflict situations, what may lie beneath them, and what possible connections you might build with your peers as you work to resolve them.

Define the problem. Create a clear picture in your mind of the particular peer conflict you are having. Sometimes it can help to write out a detailed description of the conflict, including the circumstances around it, what each of you said, the behaviors you observed, and your thoughts and feelings about the conflict.

Conflict Partner

When two people are in conflict, it's easy to see them as adversaries or opponents. But CCL has found it useful to think of them as *conflict partners.* Each may have a different view based on values, management style, and power, but neither is totally "wrong" or "right." Instead, each is a partner in an uncomfortable situation. By acknowledging that discomfort, and being aware of their differences, conflict partners can work together to understand and resolve the conflict, or at least make the situation more comfortable and alleviate personal and political animosity.

Gather information. One key to managing conflict well is to keep it focused on ideas and procedures, not on emotions. Make sure you understand the facts behind the issue that spawned the conflict. Do you and your peer have opposing strategies or tactics for achieving a specific organizational objective? Think through your ideas and give your peer's ideas due consideration.

Look for options and different perspectives. Find the missing piece. Seek advice from a source whose opinions and perceptions are different from your own. Consulting with a trusted advisor might be helpful in broadening your perspective on the situation. If you can get several different perspectives, you might want to record them in a journal and use them to help you think through the situation.

Envision a solution. Take what you know of yourself, what you've learned and observed while working with your peer and during the specific conflict, your understanding of the problem, and then imagine how the conflict might play out. Try writing a short "script," complete with lines for you and your peer. Use the worksheet on pages 46–47 to walk through this process. Preparing this way gives you more confidence to handle whatever comes up, even when your conflict partner acts differently from what you had imagined (as he or she probably will). Your conflict partner may be "off script," but you can still be more effective in managing the conflict if you've thought of at least one possible resolution.

Evaluate your answer. Are you acting with authenticity and integrity? Do the tactics and strategy you want to use to reach a resolution fit with your values? Are you willing to disconnect from your emotions during the conflict situation? Focus your plan on ideas and procedures. If you keep your conflict management plan close to that path, then you and your peer have a better chance of creating a successful resolution.

Learn from your experience. After you have resolved the conflict, debrief the process with yourself (and with your conflict partner, if possible). Did the resolution of the conflict settle the issue? Did it improve your relationship with your peer? If you can't answer yes to both of these questions, then start planning for the next conflict with this peer. You may have to use your conflict management process more than once to settle an issue. Repeated attempts at resolution don't indicate failure. If carried out with planning and awareness, each attempt can help to build an effective working relationship.

These guidelines give you something to think about as you examine your approach to managing conflict with your peers. But before you adopt these tactics be sure you understand as much about yourself and your peer as you can. Your success at managing peer conflicts relies on your understanding how emotional hot buttons, personal values, and organizational and personal power affect, and are affected by, conflict situations and how they influence their resolution.

How Emotional Hot Buttons Affect Conflict

Conflict often feels uncomfortable because it stirs up emotional reactions that can be hard to deal with. That's not to say you can't get excited or passionate about your side of a conflict. The discomfort comes from negative emotions, which are triggered because the conflict has pushed a hot button. If you want to negotiate conflict effectively,

---

Hot Buttons Online

Eckerd College in St. Petersburg, Florida, a CCL Network Associate, has developed a brief online assessment tool that is part of a larger instrument called the *Conflict Dynamics Profile*. You can use this short assessment to identify some of your hot buttons. Look for it at www.conflictdynamics.org.

The Look of Conflict

Bob was recently passed over for an assignment for which he had prepared for two years. The assignment was given instead to Sue, a younger woman. Bob was heard to complain that "the middle-aged white guy can't get a break in this company." Later in the week Bob attended a committee meeting called by Aleysha, one of his colleagues. During the meeting Bob's idea for buying a heart defibrillator was rejected as too expensive and unnecessary. He reacted angrily, slamming shut his folders and saying "nobody cares if a bunch of us middle-aged guys dropped dead." Aleysha, whose father and brothers yelled a lot at home, retreated into silence. The meeting came to an uncomfortable halt until someone else changed the discussion to an unrelated issue.

A flare-up in a team meeting, brought about when emotional responses push hot buttons, can create conflict that damages the team's effectiveness and the working relationship between managers. Understanding how their hot buttons affect their responses and behaviors allows managers to maintain and build connections with peers even when a conflict arises.

you have to know what your hot buttons are so that you can disconnect the link between feelings and behavior. One way that CCL helps leaders figure out what their hot buttons are is to encourage them to keep journal notes about situations in which they feel angry, withdrawn, tearful, anxious, or some other typically negative response. Recording your responses in a journal gives you a chance to examine them closely and honestly. This can take some time. You can step back and see that it's not necessarily another person who is making you feel a particular way. Your response may have more to do with you than it does with them. With that realization you are one step closer to an effective means for dealing with conflict because you can focus on ideas, not on emotions.

How Values Affect Conflict

Your values are critically important to your personal well-being. They are the beliefs that you find most meaningful and important. They guide your behavior and are an anchor during hardships or times of

Find Your Hot Buttons

Use this performance support tool to identify the hot buttons that trigger emotional responses in you during conflict situations. After you have identified your hot buttons, try analyzing your actions by recording your thought process in a journal. This will help you identify and gain control over how your hot buttons spur thoughts and emotions that trigger ineffective behavior. Ideally, you will learn to identify a hot button as it is pressed, notice it, and then let it go. ("Ah, there's my old need-to-be-appreciated hot button. I'll just let that feeling pass.") Effective leaders learn to disconnect their hot buttons to enable themselves to create a more effective way to handle conflicts.

Situation. *Describe the situation that led to a conflict with a peer.*

Peer involved. *With whom were you in conflict? How is that person's position related to your position?*

Peer's behavior. *What did your peer do that caused an emotional response (negative or positive) in you?*

Your reaction/response. *How did you react to your peer's behavior? Describe your own behavior. How did your peer's behavior make you feel? What were your thoughts?*

Your hot button. *Reflect on your reaction and the situation that caused it. Can you connect your feelings with specific behaviors? What other situations have you been in that caused a similar reaction? What do you think the hot button is that triggers that reaction?*

change. Conflicts, especially those that occur between peers, often involve differences in values. For example, if you suggest to a colleague that the workgroup stay late at the office to make more progress on a particular assignment but your colleague wants to go to his daughter's soccer game, that situation might cause a conflict. At that specific moment the sacrifice and camaraderie of peers pitching in above the call of duty to accomplish a goal may be very important to you, while your peer places more importance on a balance between work and family responsibilities. Depending on how closely held these values are and how deeply each person is committed to them, such differences can result in dramatic conflicts.

Identifying Your Values

Because competing values can complicate work relationships and sometimes cause conflicts that are difficult to resolve, it's important that you have a clear understanding of your own values. One way to gain that understanding is through an activity such as a values sort, which CCL sometimes uses in its work with managers and executives. Using the cards laid out on pages 27–30, you can quickly get a fix on your values and rank them in importance. To get started, photocopy the cards (there are a total of thirty) and then cut them apart. Sort them into five stacks: always very important to me, often very important to me, sometimes very important to me, rarely very important to me, and never very important to me. Be sure to put at least one card in each stack.

Don't worry if some of your values aren't included in these thirty cards. You can add your own cards with values that are meaningful to you. After you have dealt your cards, look at the stacks you've made. Spread them out so you can see which cards (values) are in each group. What do you notice? Do you see trends, themes, or patterns? Look at the *always very important to me* column. If you have almost all your cards in that stack, what might that mean? (It's very stressful to think we *always* have to value so many things.) Are there contradictory responses in this group? If so, you might be setting yourself up for an internal conflict. What are the things that are clearly the most important to you? Which ones would you be willing to "fall on your sword" for? Do you see how your values might set the stage for conflict with other people who are important to you? After you have studied your stacks of cards, record your rankings on a separate piece of paper.

Identifying Your Peer's Values

Values are often difficult to recognize in your peers because these values are so personal and ingrained that your peers may not talk about them. Using the same card sort method you used for yourself, try to indicate how deeply one of your peers holds these values. Base your rankings on how you see them acting on their values. Choose a colleague with whom you have a significant working relationship but not necessarily one with whom you have a conflict. You might notice pretty quickly that you don't know how to sort all of the values—probably because you haven't discussed them with your peer and because there is sometimes a difference between espoused values and those that are acted on. But if you think about your peer's behavior at work or off the job, or think about the kinds of statements they have made, you can make a good guess as to how to rank their personal values. It's not important that your choices be exactly right, because when you review your responses you will be comparing your values with your *perception* of your peer's values. If this activity were run the other way, with your peer ranking how important each value is to you, they would likely rank them differently from you.

After you have ranked the values of your colleague, compare these responses to those you recorded for yourself. Where are the biggest differences? Are significant differences related to any conflicts you have had with this peer? If you had been aware of these differences could you have handled that conflict better? Take a few minutes to reflect on that last question. Try writing out some sentences you could have used during that conflict situation. Your reflections can't help you with a past conflict, but they can help you prepare for those in the future. Many highly successful leaders and high-performance teams use similar techniques to improve their handling of unanticipated events in the future.

How Power and Politics Affect Conflict

It doesn't matter whether you think organizational power and politics are important, unproductive, meaningless, necessary, or stimulating. They aren't going away and they often cause conflicts between peers. For example, if a peer relationship doesn't require frequent teamwork, neither manager may

Values Card Sort

Photocopy this page and then cut along the lines to create separate value cards.

Advancement Growth, seniority, and promotion resulting from work well done.	**Authority** Position and power to control events and activities of others.
Aesthetics Appreciation of the beauty of things, ideas, surroundings, personal space.	**Balance** Giving proper weight to each area of a person's life.
Affluence High income, financial success, prosperity.	**Challenge** Continually facing complex and demanding tasks and problems.
Autonomy Ability to act independently, with few constraints. Self-sufficiency. Self-reliance. Ability to make most decisions and choices.	**Change/variety** Absence of routine. Work responsibilities, daily activities, or settings that change frequently. Unpredictability.

Photocopy this page and then cut along the lines to create separate value cards.

Collaboration Having close, cooperative working relations with group.	Creativity Discovering, developing, or designing new ideas, programs, or things using innovation and imagination.
Community Serving and supporting a purpose that supersedes personal desires. Making a difference.	Economic security Steady and secure employment. Adequate financial reward. Low risk.
Competition Rivalry with winning as the goal.	Family Spending time with spouse, children, parents, and extended family.
Courage Willingness to stand up for one's beliefs.	Friendship Developing close personal relationships with others.

Photocopy this page and then cut along the lines to create separate value cards.

Happiness Finding satisfaction, joy, or pleasure.	**Knowledge** The pursuit of understanding, skill, and expertise. Continuous learning.
Helping others Helping other people attain their goals. Providing care and support.	**Love** Being involved in close, affectionate relationships. Intimacy.
Humor The ability to laugh at oneself and life.	**Loyalty** Faithfulness, duty, dedication.
Integrity Acting in accord with moral and ethical standards. Honesty, sincerity, and truth. Trustworthiness.	**Order** Respectful of authority, rules, and regulations. A sense of stability, routine, and predictability.

Photocopy this page and then cut along the lines to create separate value cards.

Physical fitness Staying in shape through exercise and physical activity.	**Self-respect** Pride, self-esteem, sense of personal identity.
Reflection Taking time out to think about the past, present, and future.	**Spirituality** Strong spiritual/religious beliefs. Moral fulfillment.
Responsibility Dependability, reliability, accountability for results.	**Wisdom** Sound judgment based on knowledge, experience, and understanding.

recognize or appreciate the other's authority. During a conflict both may feel that their power is being threatened, their authority is being questioned or dismissed, or their hard-won territory is under assault.

There are many kinds of power in organizations. It can be formal and based on position, such as a boss to a direct report. It can be ingrained in the organizational chart, such as the vice presidents on an executive team over department heads. Power can also have informal sources, such as a person's charisma or connections. Some people have power that is linked to their ability to inspire, coerce, influence, or reward others. Relationships without explicit formal power—such as between peers—often contain channels of informal power. The play between formal power and informal power is the essence of organizational politics—and conflict between peers often debuts on that political stage.

Identifying Your Power

To become better at managing conflict with your peers, examine the authority and power you exert in your organization and in your relationships with colleagues. For example, you may have power related to your expertise in an area the organization considers critical. Consider the kinds of power you have and then describe them using the guidelines on page 33. Think also about your peers and the power they might need to access and which you can provide. Consider unorthodox power sources. You collect a certain amount of power, for example, by praising people's work in front of others. You might have power based on your office location. The descriptions listed here aren't a complete picture of organizational and personal power, but only an example. You can work with your own labels and descriptions. Record your responses in a journal so you can return to them and look for patterns and lessons. This process can help you see where you might encounter conflict and how you might fare in a conflict situation.

Locating Organizational Power

For each of the descriptions listed below, describe what this power looks like by recording your responses in a journal. Some things to think about: Which of your peers is affected by your use of this power? Who needs to tap into your power source? Who else in the organization is affected by your use of this power? Why do they need access to your power source? What effect might this power have in managing a conflict with your peers? Ask the same questions about the peer with whom you're in conflict.

Formal Power: Personal Assessment

Position. Your department is closer to your organization's center of power than your peer's department.

Mission critical. Your organization places a high value on a task or project for which you are responsible.

Informal Power: Personal Assessment

Expertise. You have specific skills, knowledge, and experience.

Network. You have supportive connections with others in the organization.

Influence. You have a personal rapport with people that inspires them.

Information. You have formal and informal communication channels that keep you "in the loop" about important organization developments.

Mapping Organizational Power

You can also use the guidelines on page 33 to create a map that illustrates the kinds of power you and your peers have and how they might cause conflict or affect a conflict situation. Such a map can help you visualize connections you and your

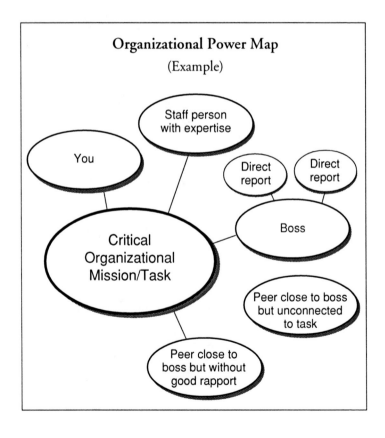

Organizational Power Map
(Example)

You

Staff person with expertise

Direct report

Direct report

Boss

Critical Organizational Mission/Task

Peer close to boss but unconnected to task

Peer close to boss but without good rapport

peers have. You can build on those connections and create common ground for resolving conflict.

Managing Conflict for Results

Do you have a preference for dealing with conflict? Do you confront conflict head-on when it occurs, for example, or do you absorb the situation, reflect, and then meet with the person with whom you're at odds? You are probably most comfortable settling conflicts with peers who deal with conflict in the same way you do. But you won't always have that luxury. Effective managers learn how their own and their peers' emotional hot buttons, values, and power affect conflict situations. These issues not only influence what conflicts emerge but also how different managers handle those conflicts and how they turn out.

Conflict makes some managers miserable and they prefer to avoid it at all costs, even deferring to

The Look of Conflict

Robert is a facilities manager at a small college. His peers are the academic deans, to whom the faculty members report. When faculty members request work from Robert, however, they behave as though he reports to them. Faculty members sometimes fill out work orders with very specific details, but Robert's expertise and experience tell him the task is impossible to perform in the way requested. The result is a conflict about how the work should be carried out. This conflict carries a lot of symbolic weight for faculty members, who already feel powerless in a large bureaucracy that, they think, fails to appreciate their contributions. They have little formal power, yet are essential to the organization. Although Robert could use the budget, the organization's bid process, or supplier selection as a means of dealing with the conflict, that strategy would carry great political cost.

Sometimes managers have to negotiate conflicts because their peers don't understand the organization's hierarchy or don't feel recognized for their contributions. In other words, because a manager's peers (at the same level in the organization but with different functional responsibilities) feel that the power they have in the organization isn't commensurate with the importance of their contributions, they do what is necessary to exercise some other kind of power. Each time this happens conflict results.

others at their own expense. Other managers want to bargain and compromise, and are willing to give up a few things if a peer will do the same. Once you know how emotional hot buttons affect conflict situations and influence behavior, and you understand how differences in values and power play out on both sides of a conflict, you can develop a plan for effectively managing conflict with your peers. And that will lead to effective working relationships that serve you, your peers, and the organization.

Six Paths to Managing Conflict with Peers

◄▶ **Take a walk in your peers' shoes.** Try to understand their point of view, motivation, and reaction to the conflict. Ask for examples to clarify the issues. Rephrase, restate, or summarize what you think has been said. Focus on the other person's words and behavior rather than on your assumptions. Examine the flaws in your position.

▶ **Create a solution together.** Identify each other's motives, goals, and agendas. Look for points of mutual agreement and interdependence. Begin with less complicated issues, then work toward resolving more difficult ones. Together, suggest possible solutions without evaluating them and then narrow the choices to the best two or three. Select a solution or combination of solutions that best meets each person's needs.

▶ **Positively express emotions.** Watch out for your hot buttons. Be sure that your expression of emotions is helpful to the process. Explain how you feel and why. Choose your words carefully. Keep them courteous and professional. Don't cast blame. Express your desire to understand. Ask if the other person understands your feelings. Encourage the other person to express their feelings. Admit responsibility for your part in the conflict. Ask what you can do to make amends. If you have caused emotional distress, sincerely apologize, and mean it.

Reach out and touch someone. Think about how you want to be viewed after the conflict is over. Follow up with the person with whom you were in conflict. Take (or make) the opportunity to talk informally with your peers outside of work projects—meet them for lunch, acknowledge birthdays, ask about their interests.

Reflect and understand. Note your initial reaction to a conflict and analyze why you had that reaction. Consider the impact of differences in style and opinions between you and your peers. Review alternative reactions and the pros and cons of each. Solicit input from other parties (if appropriate) and allow them to raise issues. Organize your thoughts and strategies. Give your peer time to reflect. Remind yourself that a delay in responding isn't the same as avoiding or ignoring the conflict.

Go with the flow. Look forward, not back. Find the best in people and in the situation. Always look toward adapting and accepting. Communicate optimism. Seek out sympathetic co-workers or friends when you need to "unload" or need a pep talk. If opportunities to reconcile or resolve the conflict fail, keep trying. Stay professional in your attitude, words, and behavior. Avoid sarcasm and cynicism, and keep a sense of humor.

Suggested Readings

Capobianco, S., Davis, M. H., & Kraus, L. A. (1999). *Managing conflict dynamics: A practical approach.* St. Petersburg, FL: Eckerd College Management Development Institute.

Elgin, S. H. (1997). *How to disagree without being disagreeable: Getting your point across with the gentle art of verbal self-defense.* New York: John Wiley & Sons.

Elgin, S. H. (2000). *The gentle art of verbal self-defense at work.* New York: Prentice Hall.

Fisher, R., Ury, W., & Patton, B. (1992). *Getting to yes: Negotiating agreement without giving in* (2nd ed.). New York: Houghton-Mifflin.

Lerner, H. (2002). *The dance of connection: How to talk to someone when you're mad, hurt, scared, frustrated, insulted, betrayed, or desperate.* New York: HarperCollins.

Popejoy, B., & McManigle, B. J. (2002). *Managing conflict with direct reports.* Greensboro, NC: Center for Creative Leadership.

Sharpe, D., & Johnson, E. (2002). *Managing conflict with your boss.* Greensboro, NC: Center for Creative Leadership.

Stone, D., Patton, B., Heen, S., & Fisher, R. (2000). *Difficult conversations: How to discuss what matters most.* New York: Penguin Putnam.

Yukl, G. (2001). *Leadership in organizations* (5th ed.). Upper Saddle River, NJ: Prentice Hall.

Background

CCL began exploring the dynamics of derailment among North American executives in 1983. Results from this research have been used in training programs, assessment instruments, and numerous human-resources initiatives in several organizations. Those results also came together with CCL faculty design efforts during the creation of Foundations of Leadership (FOL), a three-day activity-enriched program that teaches the basics of effective leadership.

FOL focuses on personal awareness and growth, working relationships, influence skills, and conflict resolution. That last point emerged as a key theme during the program's design. CCL used its extensive experience in educating leaders in the area of personal awareness to develop a way to approach conflict that moved beyond negotiation or tactics. Instead, CCL asked FOL participants to become aware of their thoughts and feelings about conflict, to be aware of the influence that reason and emotion exert during a conflict situation, and to be mindful of those thoughts and feelings as a means of managing conflict so that it enriches working relationships instead of damaging them.

This basic idea, summed up in the phrase "conflict is a problem wrapped in emotion," gave rise to a process through which managers can approach, navigate, and manage conflict situations within their own organizational contexts. FOL has since undergone many revisions, but the link to personal awareness—to recognize the emotional and rational sources of behavior as a key element to managing conflict—remains intact.

Key Point Summary

In any organization, conflicts are bound to occur between managers. Because they can't be avoided, effective managers learn to manage them by examining three key issues. They assess their emotional "hot buttons" that trigger ineffective behaviors and make conflict difficult to manage. They examine their personal values and how those might conflict with what their peers find important. Finally, they assess their own and their peers' power in the organization and learn how it influences the resolution of conflicts. Paying attention to these issues will help managers learn how to resolve conflict in a way that fosters and maintains effective working relationships.

There are several helpful tactics for approaching a conflict you are having with a peer. Try to understand your peer's point of view, motivation, and reaction to the conflict. Identify your motives, goals, and agendas and those of your peer. Look for points of mutual agreement. Express your emotions in a way that is helpful to resolving the conflict. Follow up with the person with whom you are in conflict. Note your initial reaction to a conflict and analyze why it occurred. Finally, always look ahead and don't dwell on the past—find the best in people and in the situation.

It can be useful to see the other person as a partner and not an adversary or opponent. Each of you has a different view based on such aspects as your values, management style, and power in the organization. Building awareness of and accepting the differences between you are good first steps in managing conflict. Making the situation more comfortable and alleviating personal and political animosity will help move the conflict toward resolution—and that will bring the best results to your organization and build the relationships you need to become and remain an effective leader.

Ordering Information

TO GET MORE INFORMATION, TO ORDER OTHER IDEAS INTO ACTION GUIDEBOOKS, OR TO FIND OUT ABOUT BULK-ORDER DISCOUNTS, PLEASE CONTACT US BY PHONE AT 336-545-2810 OR VISIT OUR ONLINE BOOKSTORE AT WWW.CCL.ORG/ GUIDEBOOKS.

Conflict Resolution Worksheet

Imagine that you are face to face with your conflict partner(s). This is your opportunity to plan for what could be a potentially difficult interaction. Use this guide to plan for this encounter. By planning this important dialogue, you increase your chance of having a successful outcome. You can get ready for this meeting by:

- going over the things you want to say in your mind
- using a flowchart to draft your discussion
- thinking through how you will respond to difficult situations
- practicing with a learning partner.

---

1. Establish rapport and set the stage.

How can you break the ice and lay the groundwork for a discussion? Think of actual sentences you might use.

---

2. Describe the situation and the behavior.

How can you state clearly and objectively what you want in a way that is less likely to provoke excessive defensiveness? Plan an actual sentence you could use.

---

3. Prepare for the interaction.

a. Outline how the other person might possibly respond.

I.	II.	III.

b. Outline your counters to each response.

I.	II.	III.

4. Review and reflect.
Answer the questions below after your meeting.

What did you learn from the meeting?	What worked?	What could be improved?	How will you modify your script?

CPSIA information can be obtained at www.ICGtesting.com
Printed in the USA
BVOW01s1759161013

333885BV00008B/245/A